History of Natchez Indians of America

History of Natchez Indians
of America

Collection

LM Publishers

The voyagers visited the Natchez Indians, near the site of the present city of that name, where they found a 'religious and political despotism, a privileged class descended from the sun, a temple and a sacred fire.'

- Mark Twain

The Natchez are a tribe of American Indians who lived in the area of the present town of Natchez in Mississippi. Around 1730, after the wars against the French, they were defeated and dispersed. Most of the survivors were reduced to slavery by the French others found refuge among other tribes.

In an old Encyclopedia[1] we read the following about the Natchez and their city:

In 1716, on the bluff Le Moyne de Bienville[2] built Fort Rosalie for the

---

[1] Encyclopædia Britannica, 1911.
[2] Le Moyne de Bienville was French Governor of Louisiana and founder of New Orleans. (See Part I; section III)

protection of some French warehouses, and later the French demanded a neighbouring hill for another settlement. This offended the Natchez, and on the 28th of November 1729 they massacred the French and destroyed the fort, which was immediately rebuilt, and in 1764 was handed over to the English in accordance with the treaty of Paris, and became Fort Panmure; in 1779 it was turned over to the Spanish, who held it until 1798, when they withdrew and United States troops occupied the place. Under Spanish rule Natchez was the seat of government of a large district, and from 1798 to 1802 and from 1817 to 1821 it was the capital of Mississippi. It was chartered as a city in 1803. On the 7th of May 1840 a large part of the city was destroyed by a tornado, but it was soon rebuilt, and at the outbreak of the Civil War was a place of considerable wealth and culture. For several years it was the home of General John Anthony Quitman (1799–1858).

Natchez surrendered to Union forces during the Vicksburg campaigns, first on the 12th of May 1852, and again on the 13th of July 1863. On the 2nd of September 1862 the Union iron-clad "Essex," commanded by William David Porter, bombarded the city and put an end to the commercial importance of the river front section.

Nowadays, most of Natchez descendants are in Oklahoma, among the members of the Cherokee and Creek nations[3].

---

[3] See Part II

Part I

I

The Natchez Indians[4]

The Natchez were people inhabiting that part of America called Florida by the first discoverers. It is evident, from the historians of De Soto's expedition[5], that a state of society prevailed among this people very different from that of their neighbors.

The Natchez cannot properly be classed as North American Indians;

---

[4] By Howard A. Giddings
[5] See Part I ; section II.

differing widely from all other tribes in language, customs, and condition, they seemed in most respects like another race.

They came originally from Mexico, and closely resembled the Aztecs, both in appearance and habits. Possessing none of the roving disposition common to the savage, their houses, furniture, and domestic implements were comparatively comfortable and convenient. We are told that their houses were gathered together into towns, and resembled farm-houses in Spain, being surrounded with bake-houses, granaries, etc., showing a nation no longer in the hunter state, but attached to the soil, with all the corresponding effects of a life advanced a step toward civilization.

Their houses were nearly always a perfect square. They constructed them by bringing from the woods young trees about fifteen feet in length and four inches in diameter, which they planted in the ground fifteen inches apart, the strongest at the four corners; the tops being bent inward to the center and fastened with split canes. The chinks in the walls were filled up with a mortar of mud mixed with a tufted herb called Spanish beard, leaving no opening but the door. The roof was thatched with turf and straw, and over all was plaited a mat of split canes; the walls were covered both inside and out with mats of the same material. With occasional repairs these buildings lasted twenty years.

The Natchez lived under a despotic government, and it is but natural that the chiefs were lodged in a manner superior to their subjects. The following description (*Garcilaso de la Vega, Historia de la Florida*) will apply generally to all the capitals and habitations of the chiefs in Florida:

They always endeavored to place their towns upon elevated sites; but, because such situations are rare in Florida, or on account of difficulty in procuring suitable materials for building, they raised eminences (mounds). Choosing a suitable place, they brought a great quantity of earth, which they raised into a kind of platform, sometimes of a very considerable height, the flat top of which was capable of holding from ten to twenty houses, to lodge the cacique (chief), his family, and suite. The sides of the mound were made so steep that it was impossible to ascend but by steps, or causeways of earth, sloping gradually to the ground. Around the foot they traced a square, conformable to the extent of the town they intended to build, and around this square the more considerable people built their dwellings. The commonalty built around them in the same manner; the whole population thus surrounding their chief.

The house of the cacique was larger and more commodious than the houses of the people, but not otherwise materially different; though a Portuguese gentleman who accompanied *De Soto* describes the houses of the chiefs in some parts of the present State of Alabama as having had porticoes to their doors.

It is stated that in the dwelling of the Cacique of Palisema the inner apartment was hung with buckskins so well dried and wrought "that one would have taken them for good tapestry, the floor being also covered with the same."

The furniture in the dwellings of the Natchez corresponded with their superior construction. They had an equivalent for a bedstead, and also wooden seats or stools, boxes, baskets, and mats of split cane, finely wrought and ornamented.

Their tools, like those of the barbarous tribes, were made of bones, flints, etc., although copper was sometimes used. In the history of De Soto's invasion we read of copper axes or hatchets, pikes with copper heads, staves, clubs, etc., made partly or entirely of copper. They also made "kettles of an extraordinary size, pitchers with small mouths, gallon bottles with long necks, and pots or pitchers for bear oil which would hold forty pints." They made salt from the water of saline springs near the mouth of the Arkansas River, evaporating it in earthen pans made for the purpose, which left the salt formed into square cakes. Their dress was much like that of the ruder tribes, which, however, they surpassed in the manufacture of clothing from wild hemp, mulberry bark, and feathers. Mc Culloh states that fans made from feathers were used by the Natchez nobility.

They cultivated maize, beans of several kinds, the large sunflower, sweet potatoes, melons, and pumpkins. Bartram found around the ancient monuments of Georgia and Alabama fruit trees, supposed to have been planted by the Natchez. Among them were persimmon, honey locust, Chickasaw plum, mulberry, black walnut, and shell-bark. On one occasion De Soto's troops came upon a pot of honey, "though neither before nor after did they see bees or honey."

The language of the Natchez was easy in pronunciation and expressive in terms—that of the nobles being slightly different from that of the people. For instance, in greeting a noble, one would say "*apapegonaicke,*" which is equivalent to "good morning"; while to express the same thing to one of the people, we would say "*tachte-cabanacte*" To request a noble to be seated we would say "*cabam,*" while to a common person we would say "*petchi.*" The two languages are nearly the same in all other respects, the difference in expression seeming only to take place in matters relating to the persons of the Suns and nobles, in distinction from those of the people.

The Natchez were celebrated for their feasts and festivals. They began their year in the month of March, as was the practice for a long time in Europe, and divided it into thirteen months or moons. At the beginning of each moon they held a grand festival, which took its name and character from that of the moon. The first moon was called Deer, the second Strawberry, the third Small Corn, the fourth Watermelons, the fifth Fishes, the sixth Mulberries, the seventh Maize, the eighth Turkeys, the ninth Buffalo, the tenth Bears, the eleventh, which corresponds to our January, was called the Cold-meal Moon, the twelfth Chestnuts, and the thirteenth Walnuts, these nuts being ground up and mixed with their food at this season of the year.

The Natchez nation consisted of numerous villages, each of which was governed by its own Sun, or chief, all of whom admitted their inferiority to one great chief, who was considered the head of the nation, and was called the Great Sun. Herriot (History of Canada) graphically describes the dwelling and etiquette of the *levées* of the Great Sun: "The cabin of the Great Sun contained several beds on the left of the entrance; on the right hand was the bed of the Great Sun, adorned with different painted figures. This bed consisted only of a paillasse made from canes and reeds, with a square piece of wood for a pillow. In the center of the cabin was a small boundary, around which anyone who entered the apartment was obliged to perform the circuit before he was permitted to approach the bed. Those who entered saluted with a kind of howl, and advanced to the extremity of the cabin, without casting their eyes toward the side where the Great Sun was seated. They afterward gave a second salute by lifting their arms above their heads and howling three times. If they were persons whom the Great Sun respected, he answered by a faint sigh and made them a sign to be seated; he was thanked for his courtesy by a new howl, and at every question the Sun made they howled once before returning an answer. When they took their leave they drew out one continued howl until they retired from his presence."

From the history of De Soto's invasion it is evident that not only the Great Sun, but all the caciques of Florida, were attended with some rude state. The chief of Cosa, when he visited De Soto, was carried in a litter, wearing on his head a diadem made of feathers, while around him attendants "sang and played upon instruments."

The government of the Natchez is what especially distinguished them from the other tribes of North America. Du Pratz says: "The authority which their princes exercise over them is absolutely despotic, and can be compared to nothing but that of the first Ottoman emperors. Like them, the Great Sun is absolute master of the lives and estates of his subjects, which he disposes of at pleasure," etc. As soon as the presumptive heir of the Great Sun was born, every family in which there was a child at the breast gave that child for his service. When the chief died, all these individuals were put to death, to serve their master in the world of spirits.

The Natchez were divided into nobles and common people, which last, with an arrogance not peculiar to savages alone, were designated "stinkards."

The nobles themselves were divided into Suns, nobles, and men of rank. The Suns, according to tradition, were descended from a man and woman who came down from the sun to teach them how to live and govern themselves. They enjoyed immunity from punishment by death, and their nobility was transmitted only through the female line.

Although the children, both male and female, bore the name of Suns, the males enjoyed this honor in their own persons alone. Their male children were only nobles; the next generation were men of rank, and the third lowered them to plain stinkards, although distinguished actions might retard the deterioration of the blood. But the case was very different with the female posterity. They enjoyed through all generations the privileges of their rank. Laudonière speaks of a queen "who was much reverenced by her subjects when he visited Florida."

The nobility never intermarried. As we have already noticed, one of their laws prohibited their being put to death for any reason whatsoever. Another law decreed that when a Sun died, his or her conjugal partner should be put to death at the time of burial. To fulfill these two laws they only married stinkards.

McCulloh states that the Natchez believed mankind to be immortal, and that after death their souls went to reside in another world where they would be rewarded or punished according to their present life. They believed that such as had been faithful observers of the laws were to be conducted to a region of happiness, where their days would pass in pleasure, in the midst of feasts, of dances, and of women; but they believed that the transgressors would be cast on lands unfertile and marshy which would produce no grain. There they would be exposed naked to mosquitoes, and they never should eat but of the flesh of alligators and the worst kinds of fish.

The sun was the principal object of their veneration, and to its honor a perpetual fire was maintained in their temples. The Great Sun, supposed to be the brother of the sun, honored the appearance of his elder brother every morning by a repeated howling, and, having had his pipe lighted, he offered him the first three mouthfuls of smoke; after which he raised his hands above his head and turned from east to west, the course the sun would follow during the day. The temples of the Natchez, like the abodes of the Suns, were built upon mounds erected for the purpose. They were usually about thirty feet square and built of the heart of the cypress tree, which was supposed to be incorruptible.

Du Pratz, who lived among them eight years, relates from their traditions the following history of the institution of the perpetual fire so religiously preserved: The original Sun told them that, "in order to preserve the excellent precepts he had given them, it was necessary to build a temple into which it would be lawful for none but those of royal blood to enter to speak to the Spirit; that in the temple they should eternally preserve a fire which he would bring down from the sun, from whence he himself had descended; that the wood with which the fire was supplied should be pure wood and without bark; that eight wise men of the nation should be chosen to guard the fire night and day; and that if any of them neglected their duties they should be put to death" etc.

Though oral traditions are considered to be of little authority, and are materially perplexed in being handed down from one generation to another, we can still admit that these accounts were originally true.

The historical tradition of the Natchez was this: "Before we came into this land, we lived yonder, under the sun" (here the relator pointed nearly southwest, toward Mexico). "We lived in a fine country, where the earth is always pleasant; there our Suns had their abode, and our nation maintained itself for a long time against the ancients of the country, who conquered some of our villages in the plains, but never could force us from the mountains. Our nation extended itself along the great water, where the large river loses itself; but, as our enemies were become very numerous and very wicked, our Suns sent some of their subjects, who lived near this river, to examine whether we could retire into the country through which it flowed.

The country on the east side of the river being found extremely pleasant, the Great Sun, upon the return of those who had examined it, ordered all his subjects who lived in the plains, and who still defended themselves against the ancients of the country, to remove into this land; here to build a temple, and to there preserve the eternal fire. A great part of our nation accordingly settled here, where they lived in peace and abundance for several generations.

The Great Sun and those who remained with him were tempted to continue where they were, by the pleasantness of the country, which was very warm, and by the weakness of their enemies, who had fallen into civil dissensions, etc.

It was not till after many generations that the Great Sun came and joined us in this country, and reported that warriors of fire, who made the earth to tremble, had arrived in our old country, and, having entered into an alliance with our brethren, conquered our ancient enemies; but attempting afterward to make slaves of our Suns, they, rather than submit to them, left our brethren, who refused to follow them, and came hither attended only by their own slaves."

Their tradition also says that after their removal to Louisiana their nation in the height of their prosperity extended from the river Manchac, or Iberville, to the Ohio, or about four hundred leagues; and that they had about five hundred Suns or princes to rule over them.

At the time we become acquainted with the Natchez their nation was nearly destroyed, though from what causes we do not exactly know. They were expelled from the country originally known as Florida about

1730 (A. D.), a part being driven across the Mississippi, and the remainder incorporating themselves with the Chickasaws and other neighboring tribes; the new confederacy of the Creeks arising upon their ruins.

It is probable that their final downfall was caused by De Soto's ferocious and bloody invasion, during which for three years their country was ravaged with fire and sword, and the inevitable consequence of which was an inability to defend themselves against the hostile tribes around them, who probably broke into their country from all directions, and smothered the partial civilization which once distinguished this part of the United States.

III

De Soto's expedition and the Indians of America [6]

Hernando de Soto was a Spanish conqueror and explorer who led an European expedition deep into the territory of United States. He was the first documented European to have crossed the Mississippi River.

*

The expedition consisted of 950 fighting men, eight secular priests, two Dominicans, a Franciscan and a Trinitarian, all to be transported in ten ships. To this armada was added one of twenty more ships which was

[6] by Ventura Fuentes.

on its way to Vera Cruz, but was to be under the orders of de Soto while the courses of the two fleets lay along the same route. The whole squadron set sail from Sanlúcar, 6 April, 1538. On Easter Sunday morning, fifteen days later, they arrived safely at Gomera, one of the Canary Islands, where they stopped for one week and then continued their way without incident. When near Cuba, the twenty vessels destined for Mexico separated from the others and proceeded on their way. The ten ships of de Soto shortly after arrived in the harbour of Santiago de Cuba where the members of the expedition were well received by the Cubans, whose fêtes in honour of the new-comers lasted several weeks. The new governor visited the towns in the vicinity of Santiago and did everything in his power to better their condition. At the same time, he gathered as many horses as he could, and, as good ones were plentiful in Cuba, it was not long before he had a fair number of mounts for the men of the Florida expedition. Just about this time, the city of Havana was sacked and burned by the French, and de Soto, upon learning of it, despatched Captain Aceituno with some men to repair the ruins. As he was contemplating an early departure for his conquest of Florida, he named Gonzalo de Guzmán as lieutenant-governor to administer justice in Santiago and vicinity, while for affairs of state, he gave full powers to his wife. Meanwhile, he continued his preparations for the expedition to Florida. In the latter part of August, 1538, the ships sailed for Havana, while de Soto started by land with 350 horses and the remainder of the expedition. The two parties arrived at Havana within a few days of each other, and de Soto immediately made plans for the rebuilding of the city. He also entrusted to Captain Aceituno the building of a fortress for the protection of the harbour and the city from any possible future attack. At the same time he ordered Juan de

Añasco, a skilled and experienced sailor, to set out in advance to explore the coasts and harbours of Florida so that it would facilitate matters when the main expedition sailed. Añasco returned at the end of a few months and made a satisfactory report.

The expedition was finally made ready, and on 18 May, 1539, de Soto set sail with a fleet of nine vessels. He had with him 1000 men exclusive of the sailors, all well armed and making up what was considered to be the best equipped expedition that had ever set out for conquest in the New World. They proceeded with favourable weather until 25 May, when land was seen and they cast anchor in a bay to which they gave the name of Espiritu Santo (now Tampa Bay). The army landed on Friday, 30 May, two leagues from an Indian village. From this point the Spaniards began their explorations of the wild unknown country to the north and west which lasted for nearly three years. They passed through a region already made hostile by the violence of the invader Narvaez, and they were constantly deceived by the Indians, who tried to get them as far away as possible by telling them stories of great wealth which was to be found at remote points. They wandered from place to place, always disappointed in their expectations, but still lured onward by the tales they heard of the vast riches which lay just beyond. They treated the Indians brutally whenever they met them, and they were, as a result, constantly at war with them. Setting out from Espiritu Santo, de Soto, with considerable loss of men, went through the provinces of Acuera, Ocali, Vitachuco, and Osachile (all situated in the western part of the Florida peninsula), with the purpose of finally reaching the territory of Apalache (situated in the northwestern part of Florida on the Gulf of Mexico), as he considered the fertility and maritime conditions of that country well suited to his purposes. He finally reached the province, and after some fighting with the Indians, subjugated it. In October, 1539, de Soto sent Juan Añasco with thirty men to Espiritu Santo Bay where he had left his ships and a portion of his expedition, with orders to start from there with the ships and follow the coast until he reached the bay of Aute (St. Marks on Apalachee Bay) in the province of Apalache. Here he was to be joined by Pedro Calderón, who had orders to proceed by land with the remainder of the expedition and the provisions and camp equipment that had been left on the coast. At the same time, Gómez Arias was to sail to Havana to acquaint de Soto's wife with the progress of the expedition. After many hardships, Añasco reached Espiritu Santo Bay, whence he started with the ships to carry out de Soto's orders. He arrived at Aute in safety, and was there joined by Calderón with the land forces according to arrangement. Meanwhile, Gómez Arias had fulfilled his mission to Havana and the triumphs of the Spaniards in Florida were fitly celebrated in that city. De Soto now ordered Diego Maldonado, a captain of infantry who had served him well, to give up his command, and take two ships with which he was to explore the coast of Florida for a distance of one hundred leagues to the west of Aute, and map out its bays and inlets. Maldonado did his work successfully and upon his return, in February, 1540, was sent to Havana, with orders to inform the Governor's wife and announce to the Cubans as well all that they had seen and done. De Soto gave him further orders to return in October and meet him in the Bay of Achusi which Maldonado had discovered during his exploration. He was to bring back with him as many ships as he could procure, and also munitions of war, provisions, and clothing for the soldiers. But de Soto was destined never to see Maldonado again, nor was he to have the benefit of the supplies for which he was sending him, for, though Maldonado was able to carry out his orders to the letter, when he arrived at Achusi in the fall he found neither trace nor tidings of de Soto. He waited for some time and explored the country quite a distance, but without finding him, and was forced to return to Havana. He tried again the next year and againa the following, but always with the same result.

Meanwhile, de Soto had started in March, 1540, from the province of Apalache with the intention of exploring the country to the north. He explored the provinces of Altapaha (or Altamaha), Achalaque, Cofa, and Cofaque, all situated in eastern and northern Georgia, meeting with fair success. He then worked his way in a southwesterly direction, intending to reach the coast at Achusi where he had agreed to meet Maldonado with the supply ships. But when he reached the province of Tuscaluza in southern Alabama, where he had been told there were immense riches, the Indians in large numbers offered a more stubborn resistance and gave him the worst battle he had yet had. The battle lasted nine hours and was finally won by the Spaniards, though nearly all the officers and men, including de Soto himself, were wounded. According to Barcilasso, there were 70 Spaniards and 11,000 Indians killed in the battle, and in addition the town of Mauvila (now Mobile) was destroyed by a fire which also consumed the provisions of the Spaniards. While in Tuscaluza, de Soto heard of some Spanish ships which were on the coast at Achusi. These were the ships which Maldonado had brought back from Havana with the supplies. De Soto thought he would be able to reach them in a short time for he had been informed that he was then but thirty leagues from the coast. But his troops were so exhausted that he was forced to rest for a few days. Worn out by the long marches and the hardships they had undergone, and disappointed at not finding any treasure, some of de Soto's followers secretly plotted to abandon him, make their way to Achusi, and sail to Mexico or Peru. Learning of this, de Soto changed his plans, and, instead of marching toward the coast to join Maldonado, he led his men toward the interior in a westerly direction, knowing that they would not dare to desert him with the ships so far away. He hoped to reach New Spain (Mexico) by land. In a night battle (December, 1540), he lost forty men and fifty horses besides having many wounded, and during the next four months he was attacked almost nightly. In April, 1541, he came upon a fort surrounded with a stockade, and in storming it nearly all his men were wounded and many were killed. It is said that over 2000 Indians were killed in this battle, but so many of the Spaniards were wounded that de Soto was compelled to stop for a few days in order to care for them. Notwithstanding his repeated losses de Soto continued toward the interior, traversing several provinces constituting the present Gulf States, until he reached the Mississippi at a point in the northern part of the present state of Mississippi.

He crossed the river and pushed on to the northwest until he reached the province of Autiamque in the northwestern corner of Arkansas, where he passed the winter of 1541-42 on the Dayas River, now the Washita. In the spring of 1542, retracing his steps, he reached the Mississippi in May or June. Here, on 20 June, 1542 (according to some authorities on 21 May), he was stricken with a fever, and prepared for death. He made his will, named Luis de Moscoso de Alvarado as his successor in command of the expedition, and took leave of all. On the fifth day de Soto succumbed without having reached New Spain by land. His companions buried the body in a large hole which the natives had dug near one of their villages to get materials to build their houses. However, as de Soto had given the Indians to understand that the Christians were immortal, they afterwards disinterred the body, fearing the hostile savages might possibly discover it, and, finding him dead, make an attack. They then hollowed out the trunk of a large tree and, placing the body in it, sank it in the Mississippi which they called the Grande. The shattered remnant of the expedition under Moscoso then attempted to work their way eastward, but, driven back by the

Indians, they floated down the Mississippi and, after many hardships, finally reached Pánuco in Mexico. This expedition of de Soto, though it ended so disastrously, was one of the most elaborate and persistent efforts made by the Spaniards to explore the interior of North America. It was the first extensive exploration of at least six of the Southern states: South Carolina, Georgia, Florida, Alabama, Mississippi, and Arkansas, and their written history often begins with narratives which tell the story of de Soto's expedition. From these same narratives we also get our first description of the Cherokees,

Seminoles, Creeks, Appalachians, Choctaws, and other famous tribes of southern Indians. The story of this expedition also records the discovery of the Mississippi and the first voyage of Europeans upon it.

*

In 1682 La Salle descended the Mississippi, took formal possession of the adjacent country for the king of France and called it Louisiana.

In 1698 M. d'Iberville was authorized by the French king to colonize the regions of the lower Mississippi. He landed near Ship Island and, from this point, setting out with two large barges, explored the coast, discovered the mouth of the Mississippi, reaching the bend at the mouth of the Red River, and returning to Ship Island erected a fort at the Bay of Biloxi, about 80 miles east from the site of New Orleans. He then embarked for France, leaving the fort in command of his two brothers, Sauvolle and Bienville. In December 1699, Iberville returned, and soon after built a fort on the banks of the Mississippi. In 1700 the Chevalier de Tonty arrived at Iberville's fort with a party of Canadian French from Illinois. Availing himself of de Tonty's knowledge of the country, Iberville dispatched a party under his lead to explore the river and its banks. They ascended to the Natchez country, 400 miles above the French fort, and here selected a site for a fort and called it Rosalie. A settlement was also made in 1703 on the Yazoo River, which was called Saint Peter's. The colonies thus planted grew but slowly, and New Orleans, being founded soon after, drew off a large oortion of the colonists from the interior, besides attracting the new immigrants. In 1728 the settlers and the Natchez Indians became enemies and, as a result, the latter massacred the settlers, and over 200 persons were killed and 500 taken prisoners. The captives were, however, released, and new and stronger forts were erected. Aided by the Choctaw tribes, the French succeeded in destroying the tribe, the greater part of which fell in battle.

In 1733 the colony went to war with the Chickasaws, allies of the English, and the conflict continued for several years. There was a peace, followed in 1752 by another Indian war.

In 1762 when Florida was ceded to Great Britain, that part of the present State lying south of a line drawn eastward from the mouth of the Yazoo River (practically from Vicksburg) was claimed to be part of

Florida; and when in 1781 Spain conquered Florida, that part of the State came under Spanish rule. In 1798 the Mississippi Territory was created by Congress.

III

Who was Le Moyne de Bienville who built a Fort on the land of Natchez [7] ?

Jean-Baptiste Le Moyne, or Sieur de Bienville, was French Governor of Louisiana and founder of New Orleans. He was born in Montreal, Canada, 24 February, 1680; and died in Paris, 7 March, 1767.

His father, Charles le Moyne de Bienville, settled in Canada in 1640; his three brothers, Iberville, Serigny, and Chateauguay, likewise distinguished themselves in the early history of Louisiana.

---

[7] By Edward P. Spillane.

In 1698-1699, Bienville accompanied his brother Iberville in an expedition despatched from France to explore the territory near the mouth of the Mississippi. They founded a settlement at old Biloxi, where in 1700 Bienville become commandant, and, after Iberville's death in 1706, governor of the colony.

It was believed in France that Louisiana presented a rich field for enterprise and speculation and a grant with exclusive privileges was obtained by Antoine Crozat for fifteen years.

In 1712 Crozat appointed M. la Mothe Cadillac, governor, and M. de Bienville lieutenant-governor. But Cadillac dying in 1715, Bienville once more assumed the reins of government.

In 1716, he conducted an expedition against the Natchez Indians, and having brought them to terms, finished the fort "Rosalie" which had been commenced by his brother, Iberville, sixteen years before.

In 1717, Epinay, a new governor, arrived in the colony, bringing with him the decoration of the Cross of St. Louis for Bienville. In the meantime,

Crozat, failing to realize the great profits he had expected, abandoned the whole enterprise and surrendered his charter to the king in 1717. Another company was at once formed and Bienville received a new commission as governor of the province. He now resolved to remove the headquarters from Biloxi, Mobile, and St. Louis Bay to the more fertile region of the Mississippi River, and in 1718 he selected the site for a new settlement, which he called New Orleans. He left fifty persons there to clear the land and build some houses, but it was not till 1722 that it became the seat of government.

Experience had shown Bienville that the fertile soil of the lower Mississippi, as well as the climate, was well adapted to the cultivation of sugar, cotton, tobacco, and rice, and that Europeans were not fitted for field-work in the burning suns of Louisiana, for they sickened and died. The first plantation of any extent was therefore commenced with negroes imported from Guinea.

In 1719, the province became involved in hostilities with the Spaniards in consequence of the war with France and Spain. The governor twice reduced the town of Pensacola and sent detachments to prevent the Spaniards from making inroads into upper Louisiana, and the country bordering on the Rio Grande.

When peace was restored immigrants began to arrive in great numbers from France and Germany. In the autumn of 1726, the Government of Louisiana passed out of the hands of Bienville and he retired to France to recruit his health.

In 1734, the king reappointed him Governor and Commandant-General of Louisiana, and early in the autumn he arrived at New Orleans and entered upon the duties of his office. An expedition against the Chickasaw Indians in the spring of 1736 resulted in disaster, but another expedition in

1739 met with better success. This campaign closed his military and official career in the colony. He returned to France under a cloud of censure from the Government, after having faithfully served his country for more than forty years. He was buried with military honours in the cemetery of Montmartre.

Part II

I

About the Creeks or Muscogee Indians [8]

The Muscogee Indians, also known as the Creeks, are a tribe of American Indians, living when first known to the whites on the Flint, Chattahoochee, Coosa, and Alabama rivers, and in the peninsula of Florida.

They claim to have come out of the earth, and to have emigrated from the northwest, led by the Cussitaws,

---

[8] Based on the work of John G. Shea.

till they reached Florida, whence they fell back and took possession of the region extending east to the Ocmulgee and west to the Coosa and Tallapoosa. As this abounded in creeks and rivulets, it was called by the early English settlers the Creek country, and the Indians came to be known as Creek Indians. Those remaining in Florida were called Seminoles (wanderers). The Hitchitees, Cussitaws, and Cowetas settled on the Appalachicola and Flint; the Coosas and Alabamas on the rivers bearing those names.

As early as 1540 the Spaniards under De Soto reached the Coosas, Alabamas, Tuscaloosas, Tallisses, and Pacahas. Twenty years after Tristan de Luna made an alliance with the Coosas. The Spaniards at an early day won over the Appalaches. In the territory occupied by the Creeks were tribes like the Oconees, Okchais, Wetumpkas, and Pacahas, whom they incorporated, and whose language modified the original language of the Creeks. When Carolina and Louisiana began to be settled, the Creek nations were courted by English, French, and Spaniards. The English, establishing Fort Moore, won the lower Creeks by their trade; the upper Creeks were under French influence; the Appalaches had been Christianized by the Spaniards, who by the honors paid the emperor of the Cowetas hoped to control all.

In 1710 the Cowetas made war on Carolina, and were received with distinction at St. Augustine; but Chipacafi, who became emperor in 1718, visited Mobile and joined the French side. Fort Alibamon was built by the French and a garrison maintained there. This influence was maintained for several years, but in 1732 Oglethorpe made a treaty at Savannah with eight tribes of Creeks, and in 1739 negotiated with the Cowetas. This influence led them to join him against St. Augustine in 1742. English traders settled among them, but their fidelity was so doubtful that a superintendent was rebuked for making peace between the Creeks and Cherokees because he exposed Carolina to inroads. The overthrow of the French power in North America and the cession of Florida to England brought the Creeks entirely under English influence. They numbered then 5,860 warriors, and had 50 towns. When the American revolution began, the Creeks, influenced by royal officers and traders in their pay, were hostile; and besides minor depredations, they joined in a night attack on Wayne's army in 1782 under Guistersigo. At the peace many tories fled to their towns, keeping up the hostile feelings and ravaging the frontiers of Georgia. Congress finally resolved to make war, if a last effort at peace failed. It was not till 1790 that Washington induced McGillivray and other chiefs to visit New York and make peace. The treaty included the Cussitaws, Tallisses, Tuckabatchys, Natchez, Cowetas, Broken Arrows, Coosadas, Alabamas, and Oaksoys, forming, the Upper and Lower Creeks and the Seminoles. Yet in 1792 Creeks joined the Cherokees in the attack on Buchanan's station near Nashville, and on Cavit's station near Knoxville in the following year.

A treaty at Coleraine in 1796 made provision for military and trading posts, and in 1802 and 1805 they began to cede lands. A Baptist mission had been projected, but not carried out, and the feeling among the Creeks was still hostile; so that when the second war with England broke out, English envoys and the Creek prophets Monahooe and Hillishagee easily roused them to war. They surprised Fort Mimms, Aug. 30, 1813, killing 400 men, women, and children. The work of reducing them was prompt. They were defeated at Tallushatchee Nov. 3, by Gen. Coffee; at Talladega on the 7th, by Gen. Jackson; at Hillabee on the 11th, by Gen. White; at Attassee on the 29th, by Floyd; and at Eccanachaca Dec. 23, by Claiborne. Jackson on Jan. 18, 1814, defeated them at Emuckfau, on the 24th at Enotochopco, and finally on March 27 crushed them completely at their last stand, Horseshoe Bend. Having lost nearly 2,000 warriors and had their country ravaged, towns laid in ashes, and misery before them they submitted. By the treaty of Aug. 9 they ceded extensive tracts of land to pay for the war expenses. Other treaties followed ceding more lands, as the whites in Georgia became anxious for their removal, and the United States had in 1802 promised to extinguish the Indian title. Many were in favor of removing, and from the beginning of the century some Alabamas and Cooshattas had settled in Louisiana, and finally in Texas, where they remained on a reservation till 1872, when the government took steps to reunite them with the rest of the nation.

In 1822 the Creeks were estimated at 22,000, and still occupied much of Georgia and Alabama, and the chiefs had decreed that any one signing a treaty ceding lands should be put to death. When Gen. William McIntosh and a few other chiefs were induced to sign a treaty at Indian Spring, Feb. 12, 1825, ceding all their Georgia lands and much in Alabama for an equal quantity on the Arkansas and Canadian rivers and $400,000 in money, the nation repudiated the treaty, and on May 1, put Gen. McIntosh to death. The Creeks then divided into two parties, one, under Chilly McIntosh, favoring emigration, the other opposing it. A treaty at Washington, Jan. 24, 1826, declared null and void that of Indian Spring, but ceded their Georgia lands, except a small strip on the Chattahoochee, and made provision for removing the McIntosh party, stipulated sums of money to be paid to both divisions of the tribe. The other party retired for a time to

Alabama. In 1828 by further largesses the tribe were induced to ratify past cessions. In 1836 some of the Creeks, under Opothleyoholo, Menawa, and other chiefs, joined the United States troops against the Seminoles; but others took up arms and began a general attack on the frontier villages in Georgia and Alabama. Gen. Scott soon reduced them, and the government at once set about the removal of the whole tribe to the territory assigned them between the Arkansas and Canadian. In all 24,594 were removed, 236 perishing on the steamboat Monmouth. Only 744 remained east of the Mississippi. Government unwisely attempted to force a union between them and the Seminoles, but this only created trouble. Attempts were made to Christianize and elevate them; but as Christianity was known only as the negro slaves presented it, nothing but contempt was shown for its worship and doctrine, and the Creeks refused missionaries and schools. It was not till 1843 that a school was opened at Coweta. Missions followed under the direction of the Methodists, Presbyterians, and Baptists, and some progress was made; books were printed and a better spirit awakened. The tribe however steadily declined.

In 1857 they numbered only 14,888, having lost nearly one fourth in 20 years. When the civil war began in 1861 the tribe divided; 6,000 under the head chief joined the confederates, and others under Opothleyoholo adhered to the United States. These defeated the confederates in two battles, but in a third battle were utterly defeated, and 6,000 or 8,000 men, women, and children fled to Kansas.

There Gen. Hunter relieved them, but numbers perished; 1,000 entered the army. After the war they were estimated at 14,396. By treaty of June 14, 1866, proclaimed Aug. 11, the Creeks ceded 3,000,000 acres at about 30 cents an acre, the United States to pay $975,000, only $100,000 directly to the loyal portion.—The government of the Creeks was peculiar. Each town was independent of the rest, ruled by its own *micco* or elective king, next to whom was the war chief. Each town had its square enclosed by houses for the celebration of the great fast called *posketa*, or more commonly *busk*, which was attended with curious ceremonies. The micco and war chief had special houses around the square.

The number of chiefs in time became very great and oppressive to the tribe, so that they were reduced to 500; but a new form of government was desirable, and necessary for any real improvement.

In 1868 a plan was adopted including a first and second chief, a house of warriors, and a house of kings; but it was not unanimously accepted, fully one half the tribe opposing it.

In 1869 the portion of the Creeks who had since the war been living in the Cherokee country were brought back to the Creek territory.

II

About the Cherokee Indians [9]

The Cherokee Indians, more properly the Tsullakees, are the largest and most important tribe of Iroquoian stock of the southern section of the United States, and formerly holding the whole southern Alleghany mountain region of North and South Carolina, Georgia and Tennessee, with considerable portions of Alabama, Virginia and Kentucky.

They now reside in Oklahoma, with the exception of some 1300

---

[9] Based on the work of James Mooney.

souls on reserved lands in western North Carolina, the descendants of those who remained in their old home when the rest of the tribe was removed to the West in 1839.

The origin and meaning of the name, which they pronounce *Tsaragi* or *Tsalagi*, are unknown. The commonly call themselves *Yûñwiya* ("real people").

The history of the Cherokees begins with De Soto, who passed within their territory in 1540.

In 1684 they made their first treaty with the English of Carolina, with whom thereafter they maintained friendly relations throughout the

Colonial period, except in the Yamasee war in 1715-1716, and in a war waged on their own account in 1759-1761. They took sides also with the English against the Americans during the Revolution, but made a treaty of peace with the United States in 1785, although the border fighting went on some years longer.

In 1821 Sequoya, a mixed blood of the tribe, invented a syllabic alphabet for the language which has been an immense factor in their progress toward civilization.

In 1827 they adopted a regular form of government modelled upon that of the United States, but after long controversy with the State of Georgia, which claimed jurisdiction over most of their territory not already ceded, a treaty was forced upon them in 1835 by which they bound themselves to remove to their present home in Oklahoma.

The removal was accomplished in 1839, and their tribal existence continued under the style of the "Cherokee Nation", until dissolved for American citizenship in 1906. As already noted, a small body remained behind in the old home in the East.

The Cherokees were a sedentary and agricultural people, with hunting and fishing as subordinate occupations. The women were expert potters and basket weavers, and the men skilful carvers of stone and wood. They had no central government, each town being independent in its action. They had a system of seven clans, with descent in the female line. In religion they were pantheists, holding in special reverence the Sun, Fire and Water. Their great religious ceremony was the Green Corn dance, a thanksgiving for the new crops, and their chief athletic amusement was a ball game which is the original of our lacrosse. They buried their dead in caves or under piles of stones.

The story of a Cherokee mission as early as 1643 must be regarded as apocryphal. So far as known, the first Christianizing, or at least civilizing effort among them was undertaken about 1736 by Christian Priber, possibly a Jesuit, but more probably a French officer or agent, who established himself among them, learned the language, organized the tribal government upon a civilized basis, and taught them the principles of Christian morality for some years, until he was seized by the English and conveyed to Charleston, South Carolina, which he died in prison. In 1801 the Moravians began work among the tribe, and were followed by Congregationalists, Presbyterians and Baptists. Catholic mission schools, in whole or part for Cherokees, are now conducted at Vinita, Tulsa, and Muscogee, Indian Territory. The whole tribe may be considered as civilized and Christian, although still retaining much of the old time belief and custom.